Little People, BIG DREAMS
STEVE JOBS

Written by
Maria Isabel Sánchez Vegara

Illustrated by
Aura Lewis

Frances Lincoln
Children's Books

Little Steve was born in San Francisco. He was just
a baby when he was adopted by Mr. and Mrs. Jobs,
a couple who promised to parent him with all their
love and the best education they could afford.

Steve was interested in how things were made, and had a great time working with his dad in the garage.

But he found school quite boring! Steve soon realized that the only way to do great work is to love what you do.

One day, he joined a club for curious kids run by
an electronics company. Fascinated by the walkie-talkies
and instant cameras, Steve stumbled on a mysterious
machine that he had never seen before.

It was a computer! It was huge—there was no way a 12-year-old kid could fit it in their room.

Steve spent the whole summer at the electronics club, learning everything about computers—the most awesome tool ever invented.

In high school, some people thought Steve was a nerd. Others thought he was a hippie. But Steve was just himself. He could talk about electronics for hours with his friend Woz.

And after having long walks with his other friend Chrisann,
he realized how much he liked art, literature . . . and her.

Steve didn't want his parents to spend their life savings on his college diploma, so he dropped out. But he continued to sneak into the classes that interested him, like calligraphy, which taught him the art of writing beautifully.

He saved all his money and took a long trip to India.
Practicing meditation, Steve learned not to worry about
yesterday or tomorrow, and to focus on today. He knew
that one day, everything he had learned would connect.

Back in California, Steve went to see his friend Woz, who was busy working on a home-made computer.

Steve thought it would be great if everyone could have a computer at home. He and Woz decided to start a business together.

They gave their company the name of a fruit: "Apple."
Steve's garage became their headquarters. They spent
long days and nights programming and imagining
what a "personal computer" might look like.

Woz was the genius engineer, but it was Steve's idea to make computers simple and easy to use.

Soon, they went from selling 200 computers
to becoming a super successful company.

Steve knew that great things are never done by one person, but by a team of people. He hired the most talented artists, designers, and engineers, and challenged them to think differently to create the most extraordinary devices.

Whether it was a computer or a mobile phone, Steve showed the world that design is not just about how things look, but about how they work, too. For him, good design should help make life easier for everyone.

2001

And little Steve became one of the most successful entrepreneurs the world has ever seen—a hero in everyday technology. All this, just by having the courage to follow his heart . . . and his intuition.

STEVE JOBS

(Born 1955 • Died 2011)

1977

1981

Steve was born in San Francisco, California, in 1955. His birth parents chose to place him for adoption when he was a baby, and Steve became part of the Jobs family, son to Paul and Clara. Paul was a machinist and encouraged his young son to join him in his garage workshop each day after school. Together, they took apart everyday objects like radios and put them back together, learning how each one was made. Aged 12, at summer camp, Jobs fell in love with a machine called a computer—which was, at that time, big enough to fill a room. Later that year, he became friends with Steve Wozniak, with whom he bonded over a love for electronics. Wozniak was a few years older than Jobs, and a student in engineering. After graduating from high school, Jobs went to Reed College but found the

1983   2007

classes boring, and soon dropped out. Taking a job with the video game maker
Atari, he saved money to travel. He visited India where much of the philosophy
he was reading was put into practice by the Zen Buddhists he met. When
Jobs returned to California, he took this new way of thinking with him. At that
point, Wozniak was working for Hewlett-Packard, designing his own personal
computer in his spare time. Jobs suggested they go into business together,
sharing his vision that every person should have access to a computer from
the comfort of their home. Built in the Jobs's garage, the "Apple 1" was made.
It was the first of its kind, and the beginning of one of the most successful
technology companies of all time. Years later, Jobs suffered from cancer, and
died aged 56. His vision and courage "to follow your intuition" lives on today.

Want to find out more about **Steve Jobs?**

Have a read of these great books:

Who was Steve Jobs? by Pam Pollack

The Extraordinary Life of Steve Jobs by Craig Barr-Green

Brimming with creative inspiration, how-to projects, and useful information to enrich your everyday life, Quarto Knows is a favourite destination for those pursuing their interests and passions. Visit our site and dig deeper with our books into your area of interest: Quarto Creates, Quarto Cooks, Quarto Homes, Quarto Lives, Quarto Drives, Quarto Explores, Quarto Gifts, or Quarto Kids.

Concept and text © 2020 Maria Isabel Sánchez Vegara. Illustrations © 2020 Aura Lewis.

First Published in the US in 2020 by Frances Lincoln Children's Books, an imprint of The Quarto Group.

Quarto Boston North Shore, 100 Cummings Center, Suite 265D, Beverly, MA 01915, USA

Tel: +1 978-282-9590 Fax: +1 978-283-2742 **www.QuartoKnows.com**

Series first published in Spain in 2020 under the series title Pequeño & Grande by Alba Editorial, s.l.u., Baixada de Sant Miquel, 1, 08002 Barcelona. www.albaeditorial.es

All rights reserved.

Published by arrangement with Alba Editorial, s.l.u.

This book has not been authorized or endorsed by Steve Jobs. Any mistakes herein are the fault of the publishers, who will be happy to rectify them on a future printing.

All rights reserved.

No part of this publication may be reproduced, stored in a retrieval system, or transmitted, in any form, or by any means, electrical, mechanical, photocopying, recording or otherwise without the prior written permission of the publisher or a licence permitting restricted copying.

ISBN 978-0-7112-4577-8

Set in Futura BT.

Published by Katie Cotton • Designed by Karissa Santos

Edited by Rachel Williams and Katy Flint • Production by Nikki Ingram

Manufactured in Guangdong, China CC072020

1 3 5 7 9 8 6 4 2

Photographic acknowledgements (pages 28-29, from left to right) 1. Jobs & Wozniak At The West Coast Computer Faire, 1977. Tom Munnecke/Getty Images Steve Jobs & Apple II, 1981. 2. Ted Thai/The LIFE Picture Collection via Getty Images Apple computer Chrmn. 3. Steve Jobs w. new LISA computer during press preview, 1983. Ted Thai/The LIFE Picture Collection via Getty Images 4. Chief Executive Officer of Apple, Steve Jobs, 2007. SHAUN CURRY/AFP via Getty Images

Collect the
Little People, BIG DREAMS series:

FRIDA KAHLO

ISBN: 978-1-84780-783-0

COCO CHANEL

ISBN: 978-1-84780-784-7

MAYA ANGELOU
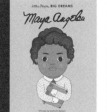
ISBN: 978-1-84780-889-9

AMELIA EARHART

ISBN: 978-1-84780-888-2

AGATHA CHRISTIE

ISBN: 978-1-84780-960-5

MARIE CURIE

ISBN: 978-1-84780-962-9

ROSA PARKS

ISBN: 978-1-78603-018-4

AUDREY HEPBURN

ISBN: 978-1-78603-053-5

EMMELINE PANKHURST

ISBN: 978-1-78603-020-7

ELLA FITZGERALD

ISBN: 978-1-78603-087-0

ADA LOVELACE

ISBN: 978-1-78603-076-4

JANE AUSTEN

ISBN: 978-1-78603-120-4

GEORGIA O'KEEFFE

ISBN: 978-1-78603-122-8

HARRIET TUBMAN

ISBN: 978-1-78603-227-0

ANNE FRANK

ISBN: 978-1-78603-229-4

MOTHER TERESA

ISBN: 978-1-78603-230-0

JOSEPHINE BAKER

ISBN: 978-1-78603-228-7

L. M. MONTGOMERY

ISBN: 978-1-78603-233-1

JANE GOODALL

ISBN: 978-1-78603-231-7

SIMONE DE BEAUVOIR

ISBN: 978-1-78603-232-4

MUHAMMAD ALI
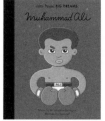
ISBN: 978-1-78603-331-4

STEPHEN HAWKING

ISBN: 978-1-78603-333-8

MARIA MONTESSORI

ISBN: 978-1-78603-755-8

VIVIENNE WESTWOOD

ISBN: 978-1-78603-757-2

MAHATMA GANDHI

ISBN: 978-1-78603-787-9

DAVID BOWIE

ISBN: 978-1-78603-332-1

WILMA RUDOLPH

ISBN: 978-1-78603-751-0

DOLLY PARTON
ISBN: 978-1-78603-760-2

BRUCE LEE
ISBN: 978-1-78603-789-3

RUDOLF NUREYEV

ISBN: 978-1-78603-791-6

ZAHA HADID

ISBN: 978-1-78603-745-9

MARY SHELLEY

ISBN: 978-1-78603-748-0

MARTIN LUTHER KING JR.

ISBN: 978-0-7112-4567-9

DAVID ATTENBOROUGH
ISBN: 978-0-7112-4564-8

ASTRID LINDGREN
ISBN: 978-0-7112-5217-2

EVONNE GOOLAGONG

ISBN: 978-0-7112-4586-1

BOB DYLAN

ISBN: 978-0-7112-4675-1

ALAN TURING
ISBN: 978-0-7112-4678-2

BILLIE JEAN KING

ISBN: 978-0-7112-4693-5

GRETA THUNBERG

ISBN: 978-0-7112-5645-3

JESSE OWENS

ISBN: 978-0-7112-4583-9

JEAN-MICHEL BASQUIAT

ISBN: 978-0-7112-4580-8

ARETHA FRANKLIN

ISBN: 978-0-7112-4686-7

CORAZON AQUINO

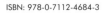
ISBN: 978-0-7112-4684-3

PELÉ

ISBN: 978-0-7112-4573-0

ERNEST SHACKLETON

ISBN: 978-0-7112-4571-6

STEVE JOBS

ISBN: 978-0-7112-4577-8

AYRTON SENNA

ISBN: 978-0-7112-4672-0